Swift

AF528461

SUR SHREE

BlueRose ONE
Stories Matter

© Sur Shree 2022

All rights reserved

All rights reserved by author. No part of this publication may be reproduced, stored in a retrieval system or transmitted in any form or by any means, electronic, mechanical, photocopying, recording or otherwise, without the prior permission of the author.

Although every precaution has been taken to verify the accuracy of the information contained herein, the author and publisher assume no responsibility for any errors or omissions. No liability is assumed for damages that may result from the use of information contained within.

First Published in December 2022

ISBN: 978-93-5628-696-2

BLUEROSE PUBLISHERS

www.BlueRoseONE.com

info@bluerosepublishers.com

+91 8882 898 898

Cover Design:

Muskan

Typographic Design:

Tanya Raj Upadhyay

Distributed by: BlueRose, Amazon, Flipkart

"Yo māṁ paśhyati sarvatra sarvaṁ cha mayi paśhyati

tasyāhaṁ na praṇaśhyāmi sa cha me na praṇaśhyati"

Bhagavad Gita: Chapter 6, Verse 30

For those who see me every where and see all things in me,

I am never lost, nor they are lost to me.'

TO G.P.Vidyarthi

My grand father

Educationist, social worker

The man of principles, decipline and values.

The one with kind heart, learned mind and poetic soul.

The one to listen melody in my first cry,

which hinted the world to name me

'Sur Shree'

PREFACE

This book is a collection of poems and poetries each and every display my soul, my heartbeats in words.

The grace of God been this much far with me, and those all experiences, people from my life which ever effected my emotions, were the motivation to write.

Sometimes it was the smallest happiness and silliest sadness, but were effective enough to make my heart say few poetries.

The sun, the moon, the birds, the rain, all collectively inspired me to write. Whereas my eyes do admire humanely things too, so many people, different heads with different ideas, every heart with its own rate of gains and pains, Society's acceptance and evils, I let my self free to feel more and more, collecting inspirations to be expressed in my words.

It's a courageous to share my writings as they all are the outlines of me as a person, as a society animal, as a girl in her twenties, as an observer, as a writer!

In the book there are some extracts and quotes too.

At some places I do have mentioned about the relevance and idea behind the compositions, so that you can connect to my words.

It will be such a bliss for me if any of my line could be relatable to you!

Love,
Sur Shree

"It's so comforting to be in the lap of illusion than tossing in the world of reality, reeling in pain and bleeding incessantly.

Beautiful poem with fine manifestation of your feelings. Wishing you grand success in life."

~ Maya Dubey

Academician

"I am feeling very happy that your poetry collection is going to be published. When one experiences nature up close with a pure heart, feels it and lives in it, then only such a living and mind-touching creation is created. Each petal of your collection reflects your pure and sensitive heart.

It is a prayer to God that your pen may attain infinite heights while moving like this,

best wishes."

~P. Vikram, Principal (B.R. Education Center, Kanpur)

"I have known Sur Shree since she was a day old and I held her in my own hands. It feels as if it was yesterday when I gifted her first set of novels, the "Immortals" series by Amish and today when I am reading her first poem collection, I feel elated to see how far she has come. This compilation is a reflection of her formative years as she faces the brave new world. The emotions are raw and unfiltered. The wordings forthcoming and chic, befitting a teenager. But deep down she has touched notes of surreal experiences and most intimate feelings which most people fail to recognize and express. While going through 'Swift' the reader will surely be able to phase out the cacophony of the trials and tribulations of daily life and take a moment to ponder upon and rediscover their emotional self. It requires a great deal of courage and confidence to present the most raw and unfiltered emotions in a way that others can connect with it. I congratulate her for that.

Swifts are unremittingly arboreal birds having no feet and spend most of their lives flying in the air except when resting in their mud colonies. At first glance, they appear to be restless and sedulously engaged. But to be an acrobatic miracle like a swift requires stable mind and an acute control of the senses. Similarly, this collection of poems appears to deal with the fleeting emotions of a teenage mind but remains anchored in the depth and range of author's own experiences. I wish her all the best in future endeavors and pray to God that the flight of the swift may soar higher and wider."

~Pradyumn Gaurav, IFS

“The book with every page unfolds the journey of someone to everyone from land to sea and the gargantuan universe in Very subtle way, reading it one can be in the world of imagination and bygone without worry and trepidation

A wonderful and fascinating read for the intrigued mind

With Warm Regards”
Major Md Asif Ahmad

“Shree's writings are so fresh and the poetries do project the dancer's soul.

The rhythm can be felt in her words.”

~ Jyoti Chauhan
Kathak dancer, trainer and choreographer

“कविता अपने आप में ही एक ख़ूबसूरत शब्द है जिसके मायने बहुत खास है। कई बार महबूब का चेहरा कविता में होता है तो कई बार समाज ही कविता बन जाती है, कुल मिलाकर वो तमाम चीज़ें जिन्हें आप समझकर कुछ शानदार हासिल कर सकते हैं वह कविता से संभव है। कुछ ऐसी ही नई कविताओं की रचना की है Sur Shree ने , जो एक खूबसूरत किताब "Swift" का रूप ले चुकी है। मौका लगे तो पन्ने जरूर पलटिए।“

~Priyesh Sinha,
Artist, T.V. Host, Comedian
(India’s Laughter Champion, Laughter Challenge)

"I enjoyed reading your content. Keep doing your best work and hope to see more of your writings in the future"

~ Manas Pandey
Geologist

'Your classy taste in literature, is now sprouting from your pen.

May all your words fly high with the wings of truth.'

~ Mansi Dwivedi,

Youth icon and a dedicated volunteer in Parivartan

"Ehem, I've no idea what to right... To be more specific what to right "good about her" ha-ha. But apart from the joke, I have seen her dedication, her love for literature and that's what's going to take her real far. I've witnessed the time, the efforts, and hours of work that has been put into this book. As a close one to her I know her love for poems from early teenage to being an adult this was the only thing that never changed. So, I can assure one thing fully that all of her writings are straight from her heart and I personally love all of them but still my favorite would be "Speechless" as I know the backstory of it. In the end, I would just say that I am pretty proud of her this time as it's her first book and I hope in future she can gain the recognition and love that she deserves."

~ Swasti Singh,

Scholar, creative head.

As you are good writer with innovative ideas and your creativity in implementation is amazing.

Wonderful girl with positive thoughts.

Want to see your poetries...ki tumhari

poteries sab tak pahunche my heartiest blessing.

~ Preeti Singh Parihar
Associate Agency Development Manager, Max Life Insurance

TABLE OF CONTENTS

1. SWIFT

OH breeze!
do come,
to my ears.

You carry
Voices,
fears and
tears.

Pain is numb.
Gossips blare.
Keep it in,
you better not share.

"Perfect" mode
is sung as an ode.
Is there a frog?
Ney!
that's too a toad.

Oh! Swifty!
Dillydally!
Come this way,
take my blessings-
“May all be gay!”

You better start this
from today's morning,
touching,
patting,
that stooped shoulder kid.
Fear for teachers.
Few! exams of the mid!

Lead your way to the woods.
You can dance,
shaking hands to trees.
When you hear,
praying whispers,
sweetly swift her sweat.
Goal of mine u just met!

After noon
don't wait for the moon.
Creep inside 17th floor
he overworked
and a-lone!
that person now seeks your way
just sit next to him,
nothing you have to say.

Night with white showers,
blasts and booms.
Stand father and daughter,

holding white blooms.
She can't find teddy.
Lost the balloon.
" Sleepy sleepy Mumma,
Please get up soon! "

Great job you done !
Come back to me.
Munch on leaf,
have a sip of tea.

Give me some live updates
of the see!
What?
Dolphins are celebrating
that ...
mermaids don't have knee!

Dear reader,

The breeze of monsoon was humid enough to convince me with thought that it's the tears and cries of many suffering souls, so as I can't reach to all and every, I offered my concern and feelings through the help of the breeze as it is not confined in any boundaries.

The poem here is about the breeze 'swift' being messenger.

2. CLACKETY CLACK

sitting at the window seat,
of my life;
as I moved forward,
things left behind.

Cheering-sobbing-laughing,
making lots of sound.
passing through woods, field,
and twinkling town.

Coal of karma,
deciding the speed.
Smokey sins vanish soon,
hearable whistle of deed!

Co-passengers varies accordingly
as the change of route;
gents board from one station,
other some robbers,
for crimes and loot.

no one knows
how long they have to go
journey became shorter
if friend became foe.
Many wish, it to be longer;
some only want to enjoy.

TTE is your own breath.
oh! it's final stoppage?
when you die!

Whether be life or
it's the rail;
some accidents easily
get them derail.

But as the paths are
already destined,
upper authority ensures
fulfilling your need.

This journey faces
many reds and greens
finally reaches yard,
to get clean.

Washing off dirt
and memories in the core.
Whole new body
with a soul restored.

Dear reader,

You and I are passengers of this life like a train on rail, here I tried to represent the journey of a train and life in comparative way.

"Immortality of feelings,
is what poetries ensure."
~Sur Shree

3. FADED HOPES

Spider knitted web,
on dark dusty pages.

Crime in plank times,
judgment in ages.

Happy days burdens,
night splashing sludges

Guilt in goodbyes,
sorrow in message.

Angle reached heaven
with wide white wings,
wings to fly
beyond world's edges.

Dear reader,

These lines have expression for the violence against women, I wrote so with the pinch of grief in my heart as the sufferings of victims like Nirbhaya and delayed jurisdiction.

4. DECAYED in DECADE

No rings to cage me,
in the rituals of town.

Though rusted badly
it's my own crown.

A crown,
that goes well
with my rigged gown.

This gown
showcases warrior,
with sword upside down.

Bare feet.
Gracious walk.
Heels made of thorn.

Twinkling anklet,
soaked in blood,
red foot prints,
drying into brown.

I poured my sweat.
I poured my blood.
Finally grown a
green grassy lawn.

5.HEART OF SAINT

Up there in altruistic utopia
someone cries in pain.

Hoggish us, suffers of bolivia,
grace of his, all in vain.

Can't feel sighs, smokey euphoria
grizzly tears, we say rain.

If you can feel it
as god's sorrow,
you may have a
heart of saint.

6. THREE BLOOD DROPS

Three blood drops,
those stairs to the heaven

They say mid night,
but it's just eleven.

Poppy talks something,
in voice that rose dispense

You know me a lot.
Owing smile in suspense.

7. BLOOD RED BLOSSOMS

Blood red blossoms,
on purple tree's ashes.
Burning of nightmares,
at frosty blue eyelashes.

8. AN OLD SAYING

Thou flower, in magenta
smiling with proud.
He laid, finger over it.
Thou privileged blossom,
rest felt crowd.

Proud faded very movement
ego captured its petals.
Thou flower giving,
me? Side smile?

Jealousy is a green-eyed monster
Shakespear never lie!

9. LOVE IS ALL YOU NEED

It goes faster,
few times slower.
Suffering is reserved
upper middle lower.

It goes smoothly
sail-sailing-sail.
Such a soothing,
cacophony rail.

Fogg or darkness,
can only make it late.
Destined destination,
It's final fate.

May it give jerks,
maintain the speed.
Life feels easier,
LOVE IS ALL YOU NEED!

"Love your flaws too,
they will surely motivate you
to find your version 2.0"
~ Sur Shree

10. PERSON TO PERSON STORIES AND PLOTS

Stars and moon
reminded me today.

Someone has roof
and walls to stay,
or moon light comes
directly to their way.

All are main lead
own dramatic play.
Everyone is an "I"
and other are they.

So, whenever I look,
up high,
moon feels extinctic.
Under same sky.

11. PIECE OF SOIL

I am just, a piece of soil.
Hope,
when 'the day' comes
no one let it spoil.

No plucked flowers,
let them live.
Decorate me with,
cloth pink and thin.

Don't cover my face,
let them see my smile,
people will know,
jolliness is my style.

Let my 'loved ones',
touch my feet.
Fake must stay away,
want to leave neat.

Let everyone come,
don't do it so fast.
Those from my present
those from my past.

Please avoid 'that lady',
she cries fake and loud.
I have been happy and
everyone is proud.

Put a glass over me,
caging me inside.
You already share a hug,
but some touches, I do avoid.

Do what I said.
Don't hear to them!
Everyone has a recipe,
to cook me like hem.

Everyone will say,
"Long live our queen."
Kidding this one
it sounds a little mean.

Don't be loud please
I want it to be quite
Properly esthetic,
vibrant and bright

Do set a fire,
to my soul.
Gather the ashes,

to get console
I wrote it early?
or maybe I am old.

Dear reader,

I never fear death but do fear the fake mourns, which only leave the family with unnecessary trauma. The lose starts wounding, fake one in funerals only have motive to scratch the aching hearts more and more.

12. Suffocation

I can't find,
a corner to cry,
Have to focus,
on being such shy.

If ever I,
dare to dance,
tripping-falling
have more chance.

'BE YOU!'
is something,
I can't afford.
Choice over
songs here,
have some
specific chords.

I tried to love
Cage's every bar
Stayed positive for
This much far

I smile genuinely,
for other its suspicious.

Home feels small,
I crave something
Spacious.

13. Catching THE BREATH

I will wait for
Everything will be fine
Who was on call?
Wouldn't have to define

I'll be free to,
cry and laugh.
Petting cat, dog,
even a giraffe.

Everything will be
in my hands.
My own morality.
My own trends.

Dear reader,

Every suffocation gives you a chance to breath much deeper. So, this materialistic suffocation should be taken as motivation to expand our wings with much more energetic efforts.

14. DELICATE BEAUTY

Wana be that
paper blossom,
golden, shimmering
like summer dawn.

Delicate heart,
with a sharp mind.
That soft flower,
guarded by thorns.

Willing to stay energetic
as dearest trotting fawn.
Having a side eye, for predators,
be it dusk, be it dawn.

Dear reader,

nature tell us that every soft, delicate-beauty needs to be kept guarded by its own skills and wisdom.

15. REAL LOVE

I love owl hooting,
and also cooing dove;
kitten seems cute,
so is a tiger cub.
Believe me or not
but it's the true love

Whether it's a temple
or it's a church,
even have acceptance
for a late-night club.
Believe me or not
but it's the real love.

Dear reader,

the basic nature of love is acceptance and real love lives in the big hearts.

16. Gibus Luna

In the peace of full moon sky,
stars down here with horizon high.

Euphony clashes of creek and shore.
Swans dancing at the count of four.

Moon though depletes still seems full,
Laura covering tera, lily bloom to cull.

17. Cheers to the Queens

Kings will come
and queens will dance.
Life is scary.
no second chance.

Being immune
towards the poison.
Snakes live in city,
not native to the boyson

Dying at the age of
thirty-nine.
Married to young sibling,
still wana shine?

At that hour.
Like a pharaoh you decide-
ensuring own safety,
committing suicide,

at that time
do remember Cleopatra.
People are snakes,
like poison packed in tetra

Kings will come
And queens will dance
Life is scary
There's no second chance

If you miss
your Childhood daily.
At some point,
one snatched your family.

You feel like
taking up revenge.
It will hurt
more you clench.

So, use your "asshk"
As the sord
Rapture the difference
between slave and lord.

King carved 'green' ring
matching to your eyes
four of your kids
'May met' piece of pie
'Mehmet' piece of pie

Being someone's power
is not sufficient.

When you can be
weakness of magnificent!

Kings will come
and queens will dance.
Life is scary
no second chance.

Someone called king
saw you in a fair,
adopted you quick
offered 'whole care'

You got to live,
in the palace.
King was happy,
prince was jealous.

King and days
passed too soon.
Governance is nothing
to fed by spoon.

People got a queen
mastered in the sords,
generated high revenue
loved sitar cords.

regenerated temples
and new cities,
slept on the floor
remembering deities.

But when your son
do something crazy
don't let motherhood
get your sight hazy.

Kings will come
and queens will dance
Life is scary
no second chance.

Dear reader, these words here are dedicated to the queens, the famine strength to conquer hearts,

and dealing every odd with courage, mainly these three portraits from the pages of history inspired me the most

(Cleopatra VII Philopator, queen of the Ptolemaic Kingdom of Egypt, Hurrem Sultan the wife of Suleyman the Magnificent. One of the most outstanding powerful women in the Ottoman Empire and Ahilya Bai Holkar the noble queen of the Maratha Empire.)

18. Shrouds are the Luckiest

Many stand still.
Searching lucky leaf.

Some crush it down,
with karma in belief.

I prefer myself
to do it like a thief,

grabbing what have
adding an extra leaf.

19. Wishing well

The wishing well!...
at the mid of the city
I still visit there,
Couples tossing coins are
totally unaware,

Wishes and promises
can't stay up,
they took a nap
being too fed-up.

Days when we walked
hand in hand.
passing by this well.
we used to stand.

You sliding to your pocket
handing me a coin
Me closing eyes,
" May he be mine "

I stand here
searching those coins
they hold the memory
Of you and mine!

"Acceptance of present situations
Helps you to stay hopeful for the future."
~ Sur Shree

20. To the elder one

Pardon the singer,
focus the song.
People be them,
talks write n wrong.

More and more
I learn from you.
Too close to confess
but still THANK YOU!

Oh! ...I SAID SO!

I said so,
Remembering the days,
we were kiddos
childish - plot - plays!

You, the one, who:
- cried on my weep.
Sugar loved by Johnny,
Black was Baba sheep.

Pencils you gifted,
marbles that you brought

level of this luxury,
No queen can ever thought!

Oh big brother!
immortal is the oath:
"will always be the tiny
to be fit in your cloth."

HARD-WORK, PASSION,
linked to your name
May you get success!
May you get fame!

For inspiration
I look to your face
whether art of life
or tying of shoe lace.

Success requires deeds,
can't be spoon fed.
The beads of your greatness
In my feeling's thread

Proudest sis. ever
Writing to her brother!
His godly geed,
guiding paths of other.

21. Remembrance

…will meet soon
will talk some day
When?
it's hard to say.
Wait a little.

warmth of your presence
feels so fresh.
Been a year.
But it feels like,
the last minute you were here
me leaning on your back
The canopy and the river.

My ears memorized all
your whispers,
my mind plays song of
your lips moving to smile.

I talk to u ...
walking alone at night
or when sipping coffee.
You appear beside me.
Maybe I just realistically,
Imagine you!

I can miss a beat of my heart,
but can't stop missing you!
Do u miss me too?

I will make it ...forever
as I always promised you!

22. Influenza

Perfect places.
Perfect time.

Googles feel dark
search your rhyme.

Sweet served to all,
I prefer lime

Hammer for chocolates
satisfaction on slime.

Bright screens
being unbiased.
Influential it should!
No matter if a crime.

23. Once a many year

Once a many year,
it took a plant to grow.
Frosty winds of night
and dusty dry blow.

Seasons of shower.
Seasons of snow.
Time kept challenging,
seedling kept grow.

These shady branches,
comfort us all.
Some leaf shed
but it stood tall.

Down to earth,
love and kind,
rerooting its experience
in young fertile mind.

Great grows gradually
not descended from heaven.
It requires an era…
an era of half century,
adding more eleven.

24. Matter of concern

I stopped being concern.
All emotions got burn,
I stopped being concern.

Meteors showered.
Stars over powered.
Kept searching my sun,
I stopped being concern.

Dream-filled sack,
I quit to turn back,
failure made me learn.
I stopped being concern.

25. Dark Streets

Drop of coal covering lights,
her sharp cries.
Men without soul.

Heartbeats haunting silent nights.
Tear's ocean,
becoming shoal.

26. Lusty Sorrow

A blue dew drop,
on purple lips of mine.
Heated red skin
adore to feel fine.

Drowsy avid
eyes,
search for you,
memories we had
from ten to two.

It's never been real.
Everything was fake.
I offer my sorry for
Past tearful lake.

27. My smile

A reward for all my
'being happy' efforts.

Me trying to find her.
The places
I visit frequently.

In cocoon of buttery fly,
a dragon which flies'
there she lies.

She, a magic power.
to accept the haters
with all there lies.

I ensure
to keep her closer,
where ever I go
I carry my smile.

28. Your sweet smile

Your sweet smile can make someone's day
far better charming than any sun-ray.
That sun confines him in the bar of time,
so, he can't feel any late-night rhyme.

But you are much kind,
not rigid toward dawn.
When you accompany night
sorrow seems gone.

Warmth from far is essential to survive,
but your affectionate presence,
keeps me alive!

29. Speechless

You are thankless so,
you can't wag your tale
jealous of his bright eyes
because you are pale.

Silent and coward,
when you must say.
But it has courage,
to bark things away.

Beat it to die or
throw acid to burn
animality is too pure
devils can't learn.

30. Promises

What if ever
all the promises die,
will get buried or
or fire flame high.

Promises met longevity
breathing the air of trust.
False hopes make it,
Suffocating and worst.

Promises can't promise
to stay alive
few words of love can
get them revive.

31. Roses

Blooming roses
spreading zeal,
hearts having beauty
can easily feel.

Their fragrances have
never been confined,
let's be generous
let's be kind.

Everyone is special,
is all you have to know,
accept and smile
for all that you owe.

32. Kiss

Bliss of sun kissed morning.
Earth owing aura of its shine,
leaves caging sun in dew drops,
flowers blush, hiding their tine.

All seems cheery, chirpy and gay.
I feel happy, I'm on cloud nine.
New tasks, learning from past,
small efforts, making things fine.

33. Feel-Cycle

Cycles and circles
of hate and love.
Coming towards me
line by line.

I saw in oracle;
as free white dove,
me was so happy
feeling fine.

Dawn got chuckles.
Morning lazy move.
For me 9 is six,
6 seems nine.

34. Three cages of love

I was happy in my own world.
Those socio-boundaries,
were felt like home.
The bars controlling my false flies,
were the safest to me.

But your freedom and liberties
bought me three cages of love.
occupied my mind, body and soul.
I felt distrusted and cried.

Your sympathetic words made me so.
A sad one away from joy,
deeply sinking in burning tears.

Wana get rid of this.
Get rid of, this dreamy sky.

My own cage is full of care and joy.
Stop being a temptation.
A temptation to fly.

35. Ready? Three-two-one!

Been with moon and with sun.

Some time wail, other time fun.

Few left before or after felt done.

Cursed by evils to love by none

Hurdles are obvious in life's long run.

Let's restart!
Ready?
Three-two-One!

36. Folk art

Folk!
The simplest art forms.

No one ever
claimed credits.
Mastered by even
society's nerd.

Mother to daughter
so, on generations
this literature,
winning over time.

Never been written.
Only been heard.

37. Childish

Every meow one, is a tom,
squeaky mice, all are Jerry.
Sweet filled socks,
Santa listens wishes,
ensuring the Christmas
to be more merry

Maternal relations
with materialistic world;
Moon dearest MaMa
Sun mama's son
Baby-sitting the dolls,
mimicking seems fun.

Blind pretending Dora,
Micky's club house,
spinach is healthy!
Popeye say so.
If eaten seedings,
from belly a tree will grows!

38. My Beloved

I was sitting
without any mate.
His moist touch,
turned my fate.

I gripped him tighter.
We danced on the coins,
silver wealthy pockets,
he bought new shines.

But then he boarded
Back to his car
In such cotton vehicle
He came so far?

His shroud friends
She saw, love in my eyes
She felt jealous
Hit my face (heat) twice

She burning so hot,
Drying all the blooms
Cleaning his tokens
With her heated broom

I cried due to sweat
Remembering his touch
" Oh BELOVED! come to me,
I miss you so much "

He came very moment
Sky greeted with a bow
My love, My saviour
RAIN comes with a BOW

She the HEAT
Waved him high
He ignored even her presence
She left with a deep sigh

He rained then a lot
Showers full of love
I untied, my hairs
Like wings of bathing dove.

They say I personify
Nature's usual things
Not for art,
but all is real
Moon shares smile
And sun pass blinks.

"Dare to dance,
On the graves of your fear"
~ Sur Shree

39. Old creature

At the down fall of his life
Deeper there alone you go
You should know
What to do?!
Or just wait to die

Down there its dark and coal
It doesn't count anything
Even if your eyes are blue
Everything seems black
With an arrogant soul.

Rotting at a corner
Dumbed by the nature
People help a lot!
But with pity,
"Poor old creature."

40. Legacy of old creature

Greet people everyday
being humble type,
earn blessings
Whatever you do
live it fully
Don't just die.

Down there,
it's gold in coal.
No need to worry,
things crystal clear
if, you owe,
enlightened soul.

Embrace your aging,
change the only constant,
process of nature.
Earn love.
And people will remember
"He was a kind creature."

"Sweet serve to all
...I prefer lime."
~ Sur Shree

"They say I personify, nature's usual things
Not for art but all is real
Moon shares smile and sun pass blinks."
~ Sur Shree

41. Goddess of ILLUSSION

Was known to,
only crawling.
Stayed in the cradle
afraid of falling.

She picked me
in lap of care.
Sent her to me,
God been so fair.

Wordsworth and Keats
full of flavours.
By myself?
Had joyed it never,
if she hadn't
recited it ever.

Her expressions
and hand gestures,
the beauty she taught
was joy forever.

'Foul is fair and
Fair is foul'.
She will mimic

all the characters,
be cute kitten
or wise owl.

Lady Macbeth's hands,
still stink blood;
like my heart owes
fragrance of her love

She introduced young girl,
who wrote that diary.
Mam made me understand
war been so fiery.

Kind Bishop's Candlesticks,
still have shine;
ancient mariners also
haunt dreams of mine,
I whispered in sleep
"Et tu, brut?"
I woke up, I was fine.

Parting from you,
heart aches it cost,
Your teachings
were Paradise
ignorance I lost.

42. Four thousand seven hundred Forty-five days

Four thousand seven hundred
forty-five days.
Moon after this had
more glittery rays.
Dolls, teddies, candies
swept by time waves.
Red drops, curves and bumps
restricting childish plays.

Gift for birthday
is a scarf with lace.
Freedom isn't free
who break rules, pays!

Tears burned cheeks
Eyes had blaze.
Attractive cage got
lot of awkward praise.
Soul seen by none.
Only wolfly gaze.

43. Bride of death

The day soon or far
whenever I die
don't feel heavy,
treat me like a bride.

My very own,
can always feel me,
from rest the world
let me hide.

Groom owes the universe.
Heavenly path he guides.
No Mr. perfect,
is this much wide.

44. Colours of Pride

Balls and dolls, blues and pink.
Society too sure about,
"all are same" things.

'Change', 'difference'
'variety' and
words like unique,
writers-write,
thinkers-think,
speakers do speak.

Days and days,
matching-matching names.
We pinch and feel about
being same-same.

"Sweet" the word,
tastes a lot bitter.
mind being bins,
tongue spread litter.

We never stopped,
because we never started.
We never accepted, so,
unique felt dishearten.
What if she likes,
brother's laced shoes,

or he secretly wears.
Maa's heels, though loose.

We in our minds have
just two divisions,
boys and girls
only holly religions.

A baby is expected
to be a boy or girl.
What if God creatures,
buoyant with curve.

No one ever wished,
for accepting such wills.
Straight and passive,
we gave them chills.

The words and genders
were abuse for the crowd.
Now can see them
posting #PROUD.

Hearts are blue.
Hearts are pink.
Hearts are colourful.
Accept and think.

45. Unfair

Once I asked him
why so unfair?

I was kid
you showed lots of care,

you dolled me a lot,
said my eyes are rare,

got me dresses,
beats clips in pair,

clicked my poses
in lawn terrace stairs.

One fine day
I grew up with my hair.

Things changed totally
I was not prepared.

Now I feel like,
abundant and spare.

The same rare eyes,
Now teary glare.

46. Ode to affection

All these days
been alone.
Alone much longer.
Alone a little less.

...and then one day,
she the one living inside me,
unloved from past
era and decades she
stayed strong.

Now when a shoulder,
strong enough to
carry her tears,
seems to be her own,
she wants to lean!

She the heroine.
Now got lead the drama!
The love and the dance.
The care and the song.
The hug and the poetries.
Happy chapters,
of the book for her!
of the book for him!
never ending plot.

People may put soil and
some salt in their eyes,
dare not to see
such affectionate play!

47. Myth

You will break,
if dance the floor;
if stepped deep see
water split shore!

The body can't afford
mentality is heavier.
Flexible and beauty
still, called shabbier.

Look at her collars,
clothes on hanger.
She is on her diet
or starving to hunger.

Those eyes so drowsy
he must be taking drugs.
Society asks to him,
depression really sucks?

It's the black magic
art of "see and judge."
gossips, rumours, back talks,
it's a human urge!

48. Curse

This much parts.
These many pieces.
Even the smallest
broken piece can be broken
more thousand times.

Just breathe a little.
Good girls don't fell,
for their own smiles.

Because the soul
I owe, maybe
is a part of
curse,
to be in the
grief and sighs.

49. Hug

When you felt alone or
enjoyed crowded scenes.
Struggling with your blues or
blooming in the greens,
whether been childish
or aggressive like teens,
nature always hugged you
with sun and moon's sheen!

50. A pinch of Vermilion

Good things I ruin,
I know I lack a lot.
You are the king.
But for queen?
I self-doubt.

I asked you,
and prayed for years.
To get me an angel
like you my dear.

You brought smiles,
wiped all my tears.
I dare to dance
on graves of my fear.

But don't you please,
leave me alone here.
The thought of losing you
shivers my deepest layer.

Your lotus feet,
I crave day and night.
Oh! dearest KRISHNA
keep me in your sight.

Thank you!